Beeston Castle, Cheshire, the inner gatehouse

THE CASTLES AND
TOWER HOUSES OF
LANCASHIRE AND CHESHIRE

Mike Salter

FOLLY PUBLICATIONS

ACKNOWLEDGEMENTS

This book features photographs taken by the author, plus old postcards and prints from his collection. The author also drew the map and the plans, which are on scales of 1:400, 1:800, 1:2000 and 1:4000 like those in the other castle books in this series. The author would like to thank Phil Hall for the photograph of Greenhalgh Castle, and Max Barfield and Helen Thomas for help with transport during field trips. Helen Thomas also checked through the proofs of the text.

AUTHOR'S NOTES

This series of books (see full list inside the back cover) are intended as portable field guides, giving as much information and illustrative material as possible, in volumes of modest size, weight and price. As a whole the series aims to make information available about less well known buildings. The aim in the castle books has been to mention, where the information is known to the author, owners or custodians of buildings who erected or altered parts of them, and those who were the first or last to hold an estate, an important office, or a title. Those in occupation at the time of dramatic events such as sieges are also often named. Other owners and occupants whose lives had little effect on the condition of the buildings are generally not mentioned, nor are ghost stories, myths or legends.

The books are intended to be used in conjunction with the Ordnance Survey 1:50,000 scale maps. Grid references are given in the gazetteer, together with a coded system which is explained on page 40 indicating which sites can be visited, or easily seen by the public from adjacent open spaces. In most cases maps will be required to find the lesser known sites and earthworks.

Each level of a building is called a storey in this book, the basement being the first storey, with its floor near courtyard level unless specifically mentioned as otherwise.

Measurements given in the text and scales on the plans are in metres, the unit used by the author for all measurements taken on site. Although the buildings were designed using feet, the metric scales are much easier to use and are now standard amongst academics working on historic buildings and ancient sites. For those who feel a need to make a conversion 3 metres is almost 10 feet. Unless specifically mentioned as otherwise all dimensions are external at or near ground level, but above the plinth if there is one. On the plans the original work is shown black, post 1800 work is stippled and alterations and additions of intermediate periods are hatched.

ABOUT THE AUTHOR

Mike Salter is 48 and has been a professional writer and publisher since he took part in the Government Enterprise Allowance Scheme for unemployed people in 1988. He is particularly interested in the planning and layout of medieval buildings and has a huge collection of plans of churches and castles he has measured during tours (mostly by bicycle and motorcycle) throughout all parts of the British Isles since 1968. Wolverhampton born and bred, Mike now lives in an old cottage beside the Malvern Hills. His other interests include walking, maps, railways, board games, morris dancing, playing percussion instruments and calling dances with a folk group.

Copyright 2001 by Mike Salter. First published December 2001
Folly Publications, Folly Cottage, 151 West Malvern Rd, Malvern, Worcs, WR14 4AY
Printed by Aspect Design, 89 Newtown Rd, Malvern, Worcs, WR14 2PD

Turton Tower, Lancashire

CONTENTS

A map of sites described appears inside the front cover.

INTRODUCTION

The story of castles in Lancashire and Cheshire begins with the invasion of England by William, Duke of Normandy. During his twenty year reign as King of England William founded many castles, including that at Chester. Castles were novel and alien to English culture and were used by the Normans to consolidate their uneasy hold on England. The king gave estates to lords in return for specified periods of military service, which might include garrison duty, and the lords in turn gave units of land called manors to their knights on the same basis, this system being called feudalism. The castle at Chester was erected to overawe the city during William's expedition of 1070 against the hostile occupants of northern England, much of which was laid waste, some parts still being deserted at the time of the Domesday survey commissioned by King William in 1086. He entrusted the castle at Chester to his nephew Hugh d'Avranches, for whom he created an earldom of Chester.

As first built the castle at Chester was not of stone but of earth and wood, materials which were quicker and easier to work with in a time of crisis. Before long the knights serving under Hugh d'Avranches built themselves castles, with a cluster of them on the border with Wales. In Lancashire there is a similar cluster of the earthwork sites of former wooden castles in the Lune valley. These probably date from the 1090s, when, with the help of Roger of Poitou, who held a large estate between the Mersey and the Ribble, King William II threw the Scots out of Cumbria and pushed the border up to beyond Carlisle. Roger was then given all of what then became Lancashire north of the Ribble (including the Furness district of Cumbria) and the Lune valley castles would have been built by his knights to protect his northern boundary. He himself erected a castle at Lancaster, a former Roman fortress, like Chester, although it had not developed as a town. In 1136 King Stephen was forced to cede Cumbria and Lancashire north of the Ribble back to David I of Scotland, but in 1157 Henry II recovered them from David's weak successor, Malcolm.

Melling Motte, Lancashire

The outer ward at Beeston, Cheshire

A common form for 11th century castles was for the lord's house or tower to be raised up within a small palisaded court on a high earthen mound, or motte, surrounded by a ditch from which the material needed to create the mound was taken. On one side would lie a larger, lower court called a bailey, defended by a rampart with a palisade and ditch, and containing a hall, chapel, workshops, stables, granary, and sundry farm buildings, all timber framed with roofs of wooden shingles or thatch. The basic form varied according to the terrain and the resources available. An enclosure with a high rampart (now known as a ringwork) was sometimes provided instead of a motte, both the castles of Chester and Lancaster originally probably taking this form. Baileys were omitted or duplicated and made whatever size and shape local circumstances dictated. Natural landscape features were used where possible, hillocks or spurs being shaped and heightened into steep-sided and level-topped mottes. One of the Lune valley earthwork castles, Hornby, is a classic and well preserved example of a motte and bailey undisturbed by later building work.

Halton Castle, Cheshire

Timber is vulnerable to accidental or malicious destruction by fire and eventually rots away when in constant contact with damp soil. Although structures of timber remained an important element in the defences of most castles up until the 14th century, the most important parts of those sites which long remained in occupation would gradually be replaced by structures of mortared stone. The earliest such surviving structure in Lancashire and Cheshire is probably the keep at Lancaster, which is early or mid 12th century, although it has no closely dateable features. It contained a hall and chamber side-by-side over dark basement rooms. Probably of the 1180s or 90s are the small keep at Clitheroe, a square tower containing a modest chamber over a basement, and the much rebuilt inner ward at Chester with several square towers projecting mostly within the circuit of the wall. The cliff-top castle of Halton in Cheshire, a site more suited to stone walls than earthworks, may date from this period although the surviving stonework seems later, whilst Lancaster has one round tower remaining probably from the early 13th century. Round towers were less convenient for habitation but were stronger, lacking vulnerable blind corners.

The castle of Beeston erected on a sandstone crag rising above the Cheshire plain by the 6th Earl of Chester, Ranulph de Blundeville in the 1220s derived its inspiration from castles he had recently seen whilst on crusade in the Holy Land. Ranulph was exceedingly rich and powerful during the early years of Henry III's reign, obtaining possession of Lancashire and the earldom of Lincoln. The inner ward at Beeston is defended by a rock cut ditch on its two weakest sides and both inner and outer wards have curtain walls flanked by D-shaped towers with cross-shaped slits in deep embrasures designed for the discharge of crossbows. Each wards had a gatehouse with a central passage closed by a portcullis, flanked by two D-shaped towers, and the inner gatehouse had a counter-balanced drawbridge. Similar gatehouses but with the towers elongated to make a U-shape rather than a D were erected by Edward I at the inner and outer wards of the castle at Chester, which along with Beeston, passed into royal hands when the 7th Earl of Chester died in 1237. Beeston never had any stone domestic buildings but there were many at Chester, including a large hall in the outer ward. Most of the buildings of the Cheshire castles of Halton and Shotwick seem to have been early to mid 13th century in date but little remains of them. Shotwick is thought to have had several round towers. The lost 13th century castle of Liverpool also had several round corner towers and a substantial gatehouse.

Old print of Halton Castle, Cheshire

The Well Tower (Witches Tower) at Lancaster   *Lancaster: arrowloop in gatehouse*

The 14th century saw the start of a fashion for building tower houses or solar towers. The towers at Doddington in Cheshire and Radcliffe in Lancashire seem to have contained private chambers attached to what were probably timber-framed halls. It is claimed that Scottish raids from the time of Robert the Bruce onwards instigated this fashion but their construction was just as much to do with creating towers as status symbols. There is a rather larger tower in northern Lancashire at Ashton which has the diagonally projecting square corner turrets found on a number of 14th century secular buildings in northern England. The inhabited Lancashire houses of Borwick, Hornby, Turton, and Thurland all incorporate somewhat altered towers dating between the late 14th and the early 16th century. Another building of this period on the quayside at Liverpool has now vanished. Of larger later medieval fortified houses at Bradlegh, Greenhalgh and Lathom in Lancashire and Macclesfield in Cheshire there now only remain one ruined tower at Greenhalgh and a modest gateway at Bradlegh. In Cheshire the circular Water Tower projecting from the city walls at Chester dates from the 1320s and there was once a mid 15th century gatehouse at Halton. It had polygonal-ended towers like Henry IV's splendid gatehouse at Lancaster begun in 1402. This building has a machicolated parapet and an unusual arrangement of top turrets recalling that of the Northumbrian castle of Dunstanburgh built by Thomas, Earl of Lancaster in the early 14th century.

When Henry, Duke of Lancaster, son of Edward III's son John of Gaunt and his wife Blanche, niece of Earl Thomas, took the throne from Richard II in 1399 the Duchy of Lancaster became merged with the Crown, a situation which remains to the present day, whilst the eldest son of the monarch is usually created Earl of Chester as well as Prince of Wales and Duke of Cornwall.

In the medieval period castle walls of rubble were often limewashed both inside and out, making them look very different to how they appear today. Dressed stones around windows and doorway would be left uncovered. Domestic rooms would have had murals of biblical, historical or heroic scenes mostly painted in red, yellow and black. Although used in churches, glass was expensive and uncommon in secular buildings before the 15th century, so windows were often closed with wooden shutters. As a result rooms were dark when the weather was too cold or wet for them to be opened for light and ventilation. Living rooms usually had fireplaces although some halls had central hearths with the smoke escaping through louvres in the roof. Latrines were commonly provided in the thickness of the outer walls.

Old Print of East Gate at Chester

SE corner of Roman town wall at Chester

Furnishings were sparse up until the 15th century although the embrasures of upper storey windows sometimes have built-in stone seats. Manorial seats belonging to great lords were often left empty when they were not in residence, for they tended to circulate around their manors, administering their courts, enjoying such pursuits as hunting and consuming agricultural produce on the spot. For much of their lives castles crumbled away with only a skeleton staff to administer the estates. Servants travelled with their lords and sometimes also portable furnishings such as rugs, wall hangings, cooking vessels and bedding, all kept in wooden chests. The lord and his immediate family would enjoy a fair degree of privacy by the late 13th century, each having their own rooms. Servants and retainers enjoyed less comfort and privacy, sharing of beds and communal sleeping in any places that were warm being common.

The early medieval castles, i.e. those dating from the first couple of centuries after the Norman Conquest, mostly fell into decay later on. The castles of Chester and Lancaster retain their judicial functions to the present day, although not much remains of the medieval buildings at Chester, and Lancaster still serves as a prison, having been remodelled as such in the 1790s. At Halton the gatehouse was maintained as a courthouse long after the rest of the castle was abandoned, and an 18th century courthouse was then built on its site. The bailey buildings at Clitheroe have remained in use although the keep has long been ruined. Beeston is still an impressive ruin. Of the later buildings Bradlegh, Doddington, Greenhalgh and Radcliffe lie in ruins, Ashton is the clubhouse of a golf course, Turton is a museum and Borwick, Hornby and Thurland are private residences. Several places suffered damage during the Civil War, Beeston, Chester and Lathom House all suffering long sieges by Parliamentary forces. Lathom, seat of the powerful Stanley Earl of Derby, who resisted the Cromwellian government from the Isle of Man until 1651, was then completely demolished, whilst Beeston suffered a more modest dismantling. The castle at Liverpool, long associated with Molyneux family, and the Stanley Tower standing close to it both survived the Civil War, only to be demolished later to make way for new developments..

GAZETTEER OF CHESHIRE CASTLES

ALDFORD CASTLE   SJ 419596   V

Immediately north of the parish church lies the triangular bailey and beyond that is the ditched motte rising 5m to an almost square summit (with rounded corners) 25m across. Part of the outer face of a wall on the edge of the motte was revealed by excavation in 1959. In 1286 it was claimed that Hugh of Pulford had failed to maintain two perches of hedging which were part of the castle defences.

Aldford Motte

The inner gatehouse at Beeston Castle

BEESTON CASTLE   SJ 537593   E

A 100m high sandstone rock rising out of the Cheshire Plain, once occupied by an Iron Age fort, was chosen by Ranulf, 6th Earl of Chester as the site of one of three new castles he began in the 1220s. Beeston was still incomplete when the earl died in 1232, and was never finished as intended. Enough of the two circuits of walls had been built to make the place defensible by 1237, when the castle was taken over by King Henry III on the death of John, the 7th Earl. The king used Beeston as a supply base for campaigns against Prince Llywelyn of North Wales and in 1254 it was given to his eldest son Prince Edward as part of a new earldom of Chester. After Henry III's defeat at the battle of Evesham the castle was handed over to supporters of the victorious Simon de Montfort, Earl of Leicester, but was swiftly recovered by Prince Edward after his defeat of de Montfort at the battle of Evesham. One of de Montfort's supporters, Humphrey Bohun, son of the Earl of Hereford, died of wounds in Beeston Castle after being captured at Worcester fleeing from the battlefield. As king Edward kept Beeston in good repair. In 1303-4 over £109 was spent on the castle, the towers of the inner ward being heightened slightly and provided with embattled parapets. The masons were supervised by Master Warin, whilst Hugh de Dymoke was master carpenter. A new access ramp was built up in front of the inner gatehouse. There is mention of the supply of various metals, including lead to roof the towers and for the making of "large hinges, hooks, great locks and keys" for the doorways and windows of the gatehouse and other towers. Further work, involving a carpenter and plumber (for lead roofing sheets), was in progress in 1312-13.

The defences at Beeston were never tested during the medieval period although Edward II ordered the castle to be properly equipped and manned during the revolt of 1322 which culminated in Thomas of Lancaster's defeat and execution. Richard II left his treasure in the safety of the castle shortly before he abdicated in favour of Henry IV, to whom the castle was surrendered without a fight. The building gradually decayed during the 15th century, when it saw little use, and in the 1530s John Leland described it as "shattered and ruinous". During Queen Elizabeth's reign the site was acquired by Sir Hugh Beeston of Beeston Hall.

In February 1643 the castle was occupied and refortified by Parliamentary troops under the command of Sir William Brereton. In December Captain Thomas Steele surrendered the castle to a small troop of Royalists led by Captain Thomas Sandford. The Royalists are thought to have scaled the rock face on the north side but there were subsequent accusations of treachery within the garrison, which was allowed to march out to Nantwich, only for its leader to be court-martialled and shot. It was not until November 1644 that Sir William Brereton had sufficient strength to blockade Beeston Castle. The garrison made a successful sally early in December, killing a house full of Parliamentarians at the foot of the hill. On two occasions the Royalists managed to send relief to the castle but the garrison was eventually starved unto submission in mid-November 1645. Captain Vallett and his men were allowed to march away with their drums beating and flags flying. The defences were subsequently ordered to be destroyed but their present condition suggests that little more was done than to remove the doors, portcullises, drawbridges, battlements and roofs. In the early 18th century a tenant was still living in the "castlegate", most likely the outer gatehouse. This part is now much ruined as a result of quarrying on the hill, for which a wider new access was created, probably the "horse causeway" mentioned in 1722. The site was then owned by the Mostyns of Mostyn Hall, Flintshire, but the estate was sold to Lord Tollemache in 1840. The ruins were then preserved for the enjoyment of visitors, a new folly gateway being built at the foot of the hill in 1846, and an annual fete being held in the grounds by the 1850s.

The outer ward at Beeston

Beeston Castle has a strongly defended inner ward on the highest part of the hill and a large outer ward enclosing nearly ten acres, with its defences on the line of a former Iron Age rampart. A wall 200m long closes off the weakest part of the outer ward on its east and SE sides. The sections of walling needed to take the outer curtain round to the inner ditch may have never been fully completed, especially on the steep north side, but a towerless section of wall is shown surviving round the SW side of the hill on the Buck brothers' engraving of 1727. The remaining section of the outer curtain wall is mostly about 2m high and 2m thick and is flanked by seven D-shaped towers mostly about 8m in diameter and a twin-towered gatehouse with a portcullis groove. All the towers had arrow-loops facing the field, and each originally had an upper storey. Not much remains of the northern tower of the gatehouse but a tall later block added against the southern side of the south tower still contains three levels of small chambers and indicates the former height of the whole building.

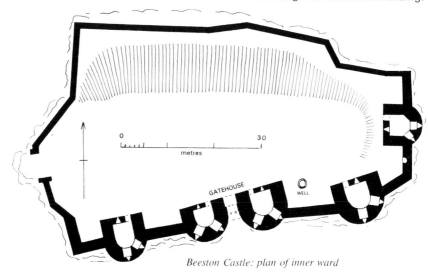

Beeston Castle: plan of inner ward

The inner ward measures about 75m long by 36m wide and was enclosed on the north and west sides by a 1.2m thick wall (possibly not built until 1303-4) overlooking a cliff edge descending almost sheer to the plain 100m below. On the east and south sides was a curtain wall 2m thick directly overlooking a nearly vertical sided rock-cut ditch 10m deep and up to 20m wide. The wall was strengthened by a twin-towered gatehouse and three D-shaped towers projecting about equally from the outer and inner faces of the wall. Each tower has the remains of two arrow-loops facing the field and a doorway and single loop in the thin innermost wall facing the court. The south-east tower has a diameter of 10.8m over outer walls 3m thick, but the other towers are slightly smaller, the east tower being 8.8m in diameter and (unlike the others) having a semi-octagonal interior. The SE angle of the curtain wall between these two towers still retains part of the wall-walk about 4m above the court and the lower part of a parapet which was overhung by hoarding set on beams lying in the holes below it. Most of the gatehouse still stands high but the rest of the curtain and its towers are reduced to about 2m above the court. The gatehouse has a portcullis groove and a pit for a drawbridge lifted with a counter-balance system. The single room on the upper storey, which had no openings towards the field, probably formed the constable's residence. Between the gatehouse and the SE tower is a well over 120m deep. There are no signs of any domestic buildings. The gatehouses and towers would have provided some rooms (although without fireplaces or latrines), but if a hall was intended it does not appear one was built. The later use of the castle as a munitions centre suggests that timber-framed stores and workshops must have once existed, probably located near the well in the outer ward.

CASTLE WOOD, BOLLIN   SJ 799838

Ullerswood, one of the castles held against Henry II in 1173, is said to have stood in this vicinity above Castle Mill on a bend of the River Bollin.

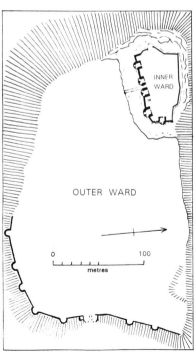

The inner gatehouse and rock-cut ditch, Beeston   *Beeston Castle: site plan*

CHESTER CASTLE   SJ 405658   F

King William erected a castle just outside the Roman walls of Chester in 1070 and then handed it over to his nephew Hugh d'Avranches, whom he created Earl of Chester. Hugh was entrusted with defending this part of England against Wales and in 1093 he advanced as far west as Anglesey, although the Welsh retook the captured territory the next year. After Hugh's son Richard was drowned along with King Henry's heir William in the White Ship disaster of 1120, the earldom passed to Hugh's nephew Ranulf des Mechines, who already held much of Cumbria until obliged to surrender it by Henry I. His son Ranulf II, who held the earldom of Chester from 1129 to 1153 was a leading player in the power struggles between King Stephen and Henry I's daughter Matilda. He is thought to have been poisoned by William Peveril, whose lands he had managed to take over. During this period the town walls were extended to enclose the castle, whilst the inner ward was walled in stone at the expense of Henry II in 1160 during the tenure of Ranulf II's son Hugh. During the minority of Hugh's son Ranulf III another £40 was spent on the castle by Henry II. Ranulph III was the builder of nearby Beeston Castle and two other powerful castles at Chartley in Staffordshire and Bolingbroke in his other earldom of Lincolnshire, but there is no evidence that he carried out any work at Chester. Ranulf III's nephew John le Scot was the seventh and last earl of Chester of this line.

After John le Scot died in 1237 without heirs the castle and earldom of Chester reverted to Henry III. The king visited Chester in 1245 and ordered the timber defences of the outer ward to be replaced in stone. The work, including the construction of a new hall and exchequer chamber, cost £850. Prince Edward was created Earl of Chester in 1264, but after defeat and capture at the battle of Lewes in 1264 Henry III was forced over Chester to the victorious Simon de Montfort, Earl of Leicester. After escaping from custody Prince Edward began a siege of the castle at Chester. Eight weeks later Edward defeated Simon de Montfort at Evesham and a few days later Lucas of Taney agreed to surrender Chester.

SW side of the inner ward of Chester Castle

King Edward I used Chester as a supply base for his campaigns against Prince Llywelyn of North Wales. During the 1280s over £1400 was spent on building new royal apartments, stables, and a chapel, the work being supervised by Richard the Engineer, a citizen of Chester who had previously worked for Henry III on the outer ward defences. In 1293 the twin-towered outer gatehouse was built, and the Agricola Tower was re-roofed after a fire in 1302. The castle decayed during the 15th century until repaired by Henry VII. Elizabeth I had the hall and apartments remodelled in the 1570s. The decayed outer drawbridge collapsed under the weight of a cartload of coal in 1585. The justices of the assize courts complained of the state of both their accommodation and that for prisoners. By 1624 the castle was so decayed that male and female prisoners had to be kept together in a room over the outer gate.

In 1642 Charles I provided the castle with twelve guns and in 1643 it was stocked with a three-year supply of food. Outworks were erected to defend the vulnerable east and north sides of the city. The defences withstood a three day attack by Sir William Brereton in July 1643. Further work on the defences was executed after the Royalist defeat at Marston Moor in 1644. The city was blockaded by Parliamentary forces throughout 1645 and the outworks were stormed in September. The King brought in reinforcements but the rest of his army was then defeated on Rowton Moor within sight of the walls. By this time the attackers' cannon had made a breach in the city walls "the width of ten men" near Newgate. The defenders sallied out to surprise the attackers' base at Eccleston and took several prisoners, but the besiegers then bridged the river with a pontoon of boats. After an Irish relieving force was defeated near Denbigh at the beginning of November the garrison were without hope. Eastgate and Watergate were badly damaged by cannon-fire and Lord Byron finally agreed surrender terms and marched his garrison out at the beginning of February 1646. An order for partial demolition of the city walls was not executed and the castle was left intact for use as a prison and stores. An attempt was made to take over the castle for King Charles in 1648, some of the garrison being involved in the plot. The conspirators were shot in the Corn market. After Charles II's defeat at Worcester in 1651 the Earl of Derby was tried and condemned in Chester Castle. He escaped from it but was executed at Bolton after being recaptured.

A new armoury was built in the inner ward in the 1680s. William II used the castle as a supply base for his campaign in Ireland in 1690. Many Jacobite prisoners from the 1715 rebellion were held in the outer gatehouse, most of them dying of cold or fever during the severe winter. After the defeat of the 1745 rebellion a plan was drawn up to strengthen the castle with four large bastions. This work was never executed, although there was some remodelling of the existing walls and towers. Late 18th century reformers were critical of the conditions in which prisoners were kept at Chester. Consequently the defences and buildings of the outer ward were demolished and replaced by a shire hall and court room on the site of the great hall. The 20th century County Hall behind it lies on the site of a late 18th century prison.

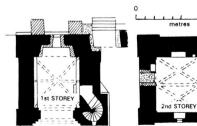

0   10
metres

1st STOREY

2nd STOREY

3rd STOREY

Plans of Agricola Tower, Chester Castle   *Water Tower, Chester*

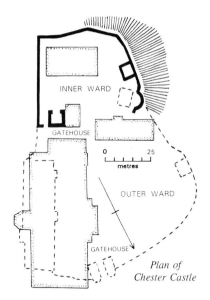

Plan of
Chester Castle

Agricola Tower, Chester Castle

The Roman walls at Chester enclosed an area about 480m from north to south by 320m wide. The castle was placed 180m beyond the south wall, a position that allowed it protection by a bend of the Dee, which in medieval times came in closer to the west side of the town that it does now. The inner ward was thus defended by the river on three sides and the outer ward on the NE side. Nothing remains of the medieval outer ward measuring 100m by 70m or the domestic buildings on its SE side. A plan of 1769 shows the outer wall with one inwardly projecting tower about 8m square on the west and a modest twin-towered gatehouse with towers about 6m wide on the north. As in the larger contemporary gatehouse at Harlech there were larger and more thinly walled rooms set behind the small rooms in the towers.

The inner ward about 50m across still exists although the walls which still surround it on three sides have been rebuilt or refaced during the 18th and 19th centuries. The sides facing the bend of the river had no towers but there were three inwardly projecting square towers, a round bastion and a twin-towered gatehouse extending along the more vulnerable sides. The gatehouse here was about the same width as the outer one but was only one room deep, suggesting an earlier date, perhaps the 1260s or 70s. Nothing now remains of it, or of the square tower immediately to the west, but two other towers survive, the best preserved (although mostly refaced in 1818) being the 9m square Agricola Tower on the east. A pointed archway in the tower SW wall, now open but shown as reduced to a doorway on the 1769 plan, either formed the inner arch of a former gateway passage, or, more likely, the chancel arch of a chapel whose chancel lay in the tower whilst the nave, possibly timber framed, lay to the SW. The probable chancel has what looks like an altar recess in the opposite wall and is covered by a rib vault built after a fire in 1302. The corners of the tower have clasping buttresses, suggesting a 12th century date although all the features are clearly 13th or 14th century. The south buttress is bigger than the others to allow space for a spiral staircase. This leads up to two upper storeys and the roof. The middle storey is a rib-vaulted upper chapel of St Mary with an altar recess in the NE wall, a window facing SW and traces of 14th century wall-paintings. The third storey may have been created later out of a former roof space. Nothing remains of the hall and chambers shown on old plans within the inner ward.

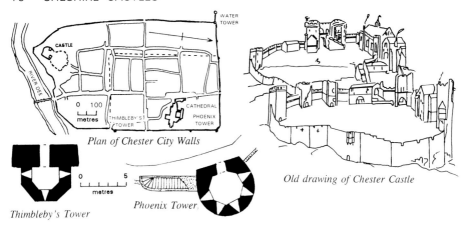

Plan of Chester City Walls

Old drawing of Chester Castle

Thimbleby's Tower

Phoenix Tower.

In the 12th century the area enclosed by the town walls was widened by 125m and extended southwards to enclose the castle. Morgan's Mount, a rectangular bastion projecting 3m, marks the junction of the Roman wall and medieval extensions on the north side. The Roman SE corner tower base is still visible but otherwise the Roman parts have been mostly rebuilt or refaced. The 3000m circuit of the 2m thick wall is complete except for short sections near the castle. The parapet and much of the facing is no older than the 18th and 19th centuries. The wall-walk is only 2 or 3m above the present level of the land outside for much of the circuit, but a section on the south is 5m high and west of Morgan's Mount the wall is 4m high. North Gate, East Gate, Water Gate on the west, and Bridge Gate on the south have all been destroyed except a fragment of the last, but 19th century archways in their place allow uninterrupted perambulation. When demolished in 1769 East Gate was shown to be partly Roman, although an old engraving suggests it was mostly a 14th century structure. It had two storeys over the passageway, the topmost having a bold outer arch between the flanking polygonal fronted towers. Over the passageway outer arch were four shields of arms. The archway of the Ship Gate on the west side close to the castle was dismantled in 1830 and eventually re-erected in Grovenor Park.

The north side of the city has a dramatic rock cutting in front of it, apparently a deepening and widening of the original formidable ditch to accommodate an 18th century canal. The Phoenix Tower at the NE corner is also called King Charles Tower, since he is said to have watched his army being defeated on Rowton Moor from its summit. Much rebuilt since his time, it is 6.2m wide and over 16m high outside. A room at the main wall walkway level contains five loops facing the field. Another room above is reached by steps on the south side. These rooms now serve as a museum. South of here is the Kaleyard Gate cut through the wall by permission of Edward I in 1275. From the rectangular Bonewaldesthorne's Tower at the NW corner of the city a wall 6m high and 3.6m thick with a parapet on each side extends for 30m out to the 21m high Water Tower, a 10m diameter circular structure containing two octagonal rooms with numerous cross-shaped arrow loops over a solid base. A spiral staircase and latrine are set on either side of the entrance doorway. When erected in 1322-6 by John Helpstone at a cost of £100, to defend the harbour, this tower stood within the River Dee, which has now retreated away from the medieval west wall of the city. Just north of the Roman SE corner is a semi-octagonal tower (Thimbleby's), 5.4m in diameter, and containing a room with three loops. There are also two small solid semi-circular towers now cut down to the level of the main wall-walk, and footings of another lie under the steps down towards Frodsham Street.

DODLESTON CASTLE   SJ 361608

Near the parish church are remnants of a low motte and a bailey with a moat still partly containing water.

DODDINGTON CASTLE   SJ 361608

John Delves was knighted in 1363 and two years later he obtained from Edward III a licence to crenellate his house. This may refer to the still-surviving solar tower or tower house about 8m square with a vaulted basement, two upper storeys, and small square corner turrets at the top. The doorway is now partly hidden below an outer staircase to a new upper doorway, the tower having become a summer house or folly standing in front of the new house of 1777-98 erected by Thomas Broughton. This replaced a mansion beside the tower erected by Thomas Delves, who inherited the estate in 1608 and was made a baronet by James I in 1622. He was arrested by Charles I in 1642 and Doddington was garrisoned for Parliament in 1643, but captured by the Royalists in 1644. From his mansion have come carved stones from which the outer staircase has been assembled, including the statues set on the outside. The old mansion seems to have been developed from whatever medieval buildings accompanied the tower.

Phoenix Tower, Chester City Walls

A second licence to crenellate granted in 1403 by Henry IV to Sir John's great nephew, another John, probably referred to these additional buildings or a moat or wall provided around them. The last male Delves died in 1727, leaving an heiress who married Sir Brian Broughton.

DUNHAM MASSEY CASTLE
SJ 734874

The estate takes its name from Hamo of Masci, its tenant in 1086, as recorded by Domesday Book. NW of the service court of the house built in the 1730s for the 2nd Earl of Warrington lies a flattened motte with its ditch flooded to make a garden lake. It was held by the Masseys against Henry II in 1173, and was still in use in 1323, when there was dispute between the Masseys and Nicholas of Audley over its maintenance, whilst there is a mention of a chapel in 1307. The 18th century mansion incorporates part of an older courtyard house built by Sir George Booth.

Doddington Tower

FRODSHAM CASTLE   SJ 513775

The cellar of Castle Park House is said to incorporate the last remains of a stone castle built by the Earls of Chester and later held by the Crown. A tower here is mentioned as being in need of repair in 1355. A print by the Buck Brother shows a long narrow hall with Norman-looking round-headed windows.

HALTON CASTLE   SJ 537820   V

The hall with round-headed windows shown by the Buck brothers in their print supports Ormerod's claim that this castle was founded during Henry II's reign. The likely founder would this be Richard Fitz-Eustace, who married Albreda, heiress of Robert de Lizours. Albreda was also a cousin of Robert de Lacy, Lord of Pontefract, and on his death in 1193 inherited his estate. Her grandson Roger thus inherited the de Lacy estates and adopted the de Lacy surname. In 1232 John de Lacy succeeded to the earldom of Lincoln. When his grandson Henry died in 1310 the estates passed to his daughter Alice, who was married to Thomas, Earl of Lancaster. Halton thus became part of the earldom of Lancaster raised to a duchy by Edward III for his son John of Gaunt, and merged with the crown when the latter's son became King Henry IV. The castle at Halton seems to have been kept in repair during the 15th century. In 1423 a room under the earl's chamber was being made into a prison and the round tower and chapel were repaired. A new gatehouse with twin polygonal fronted towers was constructed in 1450-7 at a cost of £347, the work being supervised by John Heley, who served as master mason for all work carried on in the duchy. A survey of 1476 describes the castle as "well repaired except certain defaults in the leds of the great chamber, the withdraught thereunto, the chapell, the hall and the auditors chambre, the kechyn covered with shingle, the ladrehows and the store called the hay hows all the which is ordeigned to be amended and repaired".

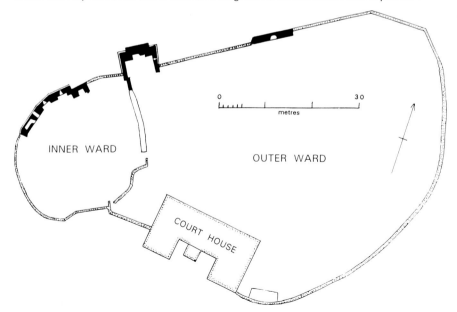

Plan of Halton Castle

In 1532 the kitchen tower required rebuilding due to "defective foundations and the weakness of the masonry". As is mentioned in a report of 1564 the castle's use as a courthouse and prison necessitated its good maintenance. However a survey of royal castles in 1609 found it decayed. In the Civil War Halton was held for the king by Earl Rivers. The building seems to have been badly damaged by two Parliamentary sieges in 1643 and 1644 and did not need slighting after its capture. A survey of 1650 mentions "one courtyard, five rooms over the gatehouse, one room where the records are kept, one great hall with two ranges of buildings about it containing nine rooms unfurnished four of which are roofed with lead". The gatehouse is thought to have remained in use as a courthouse until it was replaced in the 1730s by a new courthouse erected by the Earl of Cholmondley, who had recently taken out a lease of the castle. This new courthouse remains in use as a hotel.

The castle lies on a strong site with steep drops to the NW, north and east. The gatehouse, situated where the courthouse now lies, opened into a D-shaped court about 60m by 50m. An inner ward about 22m across lay on the higher ground to the west. The remains consist of firstly, a 17m long section of the western wall of the inner ward, 1.7m thick and pierced by a latrine, a postern and two embrasures with cross-shaped arrowloops, secondly, a rectangular tower opening off the outer ward at the junction of the two wards and having a 14th century upper window, and thirdly, a short piece of walling further along on the same side. The rest of the site is enclosed by thin and low retaining walls of no great age. Excavations in 1986-7 revealed the inner or SE end wall of the tower, indicating it was 10m long by 8m wide over walls up to 1.5m thick. The tower overlay the ditch that originally divided the two wards, which by the 13th century had probably been thrown into one single court with domestic buildings against most of the length of the NW side. Footings were also found of a D-shaped tower 12m wide further north. It was later demolished and the curtain wall and buildings abutting it were carried across the site.

Halton Castle from the SW

KINGSLEY MOTTE   SJ 534734

The very modest mound known as Castle Cob may be the site of a lodge used by the Earls of Chester for hunting in Delamere Forest.

MACCLESFIELD CASTLE   SJ 917737

In 1398 Richard II licensed the priest John de Macclesfield to fortify his house in the town in such a way that "archers could readily defend it". In 1399 Richard attended a banquet given by John in his house here, and, since it was very unusual for a commoner to be allowed to fortify a house in a royal borough, the building may have been intended for occasional residence by the king, who was normally attended by a guard of Cheshire bowmen. Having supported him during the crisis of 1387-8, John was high in favour with Richard, and lost several offices when Henry IV took the throne later that year. In 1417 John Kingsley, brother of John's mistress Kathleen, was fined and forced to return a number of furnishings he had taken from the house. During Edward IV's reign the house was held by Henry Stafford, 2nd Duke of Buckingham. After his execution by Richard III the house seems to have passed into the possession of Thomas Stanley, who is thought to have entertained Henry VII at Macclesfield in 1496. The Staffords may have later recovered possession of the house but it is known to have been held by the Stanley earl of Derby in 1532. The house was leased to tenants in the late 16th century and later occupied by squatters. In the early 19th century what remained of the building was used as a catholic chapel and priest's residence. The last remaining part, a porch tower, was dismantled in 1933 to make way for a Marks and Spencer store. It was intended to rebuild the porch tower elsewhere but many of the stones were eventually lost. The surviving few are on display in the town hall.

MALPAS CASTLE   SJ 486472   V

North of the church is a mound rising 4m to a summit 31m across. Malpas was once a place of some importance and is mentioned as Depenbech in Domesday Book with a record of five knights, presumably part of the castle garrison. The castle is thought to have been erected by Robert Fitz-Hugh, son of Hugh Lepus, Earl of Chester.

NANTWICH CASTLE

Slight traces of a former motte and bailey castle have been revealed by excavation. There is a reference to a former castle here in 1288.

NEWHALL TOWER

A castle in this vicinity is mentioned in 1275.

NORTHWICH CASTLE

A large motte here has vanished and excavations have failed to reveal its location. There are references to the site dating from the 1190s and 1278.

OLDCASTLE MOTTE   SJ 468441

On the end of a wooded spur above the Wych Brook, 0.5km south of Oldcastle Mill is a motte with two ditches on one side and three on the other.

PULFORD CASTLE   SJ 375587   V

The earthworks of this motte and bailey beside the River Alyn look unimpressive but this strategic site was considered worth garrisoning against Owain Glyndwr in 1403. There is an earlier reference to the castle in a document of the 1190s.

RUNCORN CASTLE   SJ 508833

The last traces of fortifications on this promontory site were destroyed in 1862.

SHOCKLACH CASTLE   SJ 434508

There are damaged earthworks of a motte and a bailey. The references to a castle here in 1290 and 1327 may refer either to this site or the embanked platform beside a stream at SJ 434509 to the NE.

SHOTWICK CASTLE   SJ 349704

There is a manorial moated site NW of the church but the castle site lies isolated 1.5km to the SE. Only shapeless earthworks remain of a motte and bailey. In the 13th century, when this site lay on the shore, not inland as it does now, it was refortified in stone with round towers. A keep mentioned in 1240 may be the buttressed rectangular building shown on old drawings as lying within the curtain wall. In the 1320s Edward II had the castle repaired by the mason Robert de Helpston and a deer park was created around it. The building only began to decay after it was granted by Richard II to Sir Hugh Calveley. Camden described the castle as a ruin in 1607. The masonry was removed in the mid 18th century to help build sea defences.

STOCKPORT CASTLE   SJ 894903

There is a reference to a castle here being held against Henry II in 1173. It was probably destroyed afterwards but seems to have subsequently been rebuilt in stone for the castle gaol is said to have survived until the 16th century. It lay north of the church. The town has quite a strong rocky site and may have been walled.

There are other possible castle sites at Mud Hill (Coddington), SJ 452552, Peel Hall, SJ 499696, and Poulton Lancelyn, SJ 337815. The tower at Brimstage, SJ 304827, is no more than a high stair turret adjoining an unfortified hall.

Plan of Malpas Motte

Halton Castle

GAZETTEER OF LANCASHIRE CASTLES

ARKHOLME MOTTE   SD 589718   V

The churchyard is a platform with slopes facing north and west. It probably originally formed a bailey for the motte rising immediately NE of the church to a summit 15m across. The motte ditch curves round to the north of the church.

ASHTON HALL   SD 462573

This building consists of a grey stone range of 1856 and a medieval tower of red sandstone with the original windows blocked and replaced by mullioned windows of c1600 in the vaulted lowest storey, with two levels of Gothick windows of c1800 above. This building measures 19m by 11.5m and has diagonally projecting corner turrets 4.4m square containing four storeys of small rooms, except that one of them now contains a 19th century staircase. The moulded battlements on stepped corbelling look 15th century but the plan form suggests a 14th century date for the tower, Edmund Lawrence, d1381, being the most likely builder. The Lawrences held Ashton from the early 14th century until the early 16th century.

BLACKROD CASTLE   SD 619106

This was an oval mound with traces of a bailey until the site was built over in the 1950s. Most of the pottery revealed in excavations was post-medieval.

Ashton Hall

BORWICK HALL   SD 526730

The oldest part of the building is a 14th or 15th century tower 10.8m by 8.4m over walls 1.7m thick. The basement is divided into two rooms without connection between them, there being separate doorways. The southern room has a four-light window. There are three upper storeys, the tower being about 13.5m high. A turret rises above one corner. The narrow wing flanking most of the east side of the tower is of c1550, as are the kitchen and service rooms to the north of the tower. The hall to the west, and a wing containing two parlours beyond, were built in 1595 by the Kendal clothier Robert Blindloss, presumably in replacement of medieval structures. Robert's initials appear on the hall fireplace. At the junction of the new hall and old tower are a porch on the south side and a staircase on the north side. Although the gatehouse looks Elizabethan it is dated 1650.

BRADLEGH OLD HALL   SJ 572948

Sir Piers Legh of Lyme, whose father was executed by Henry IV in 1399 as a supporter of the deposed Richard II, obtained the manor of Bradlegh (then in Lancashire but now in Cheshire) by marrying the sister of John Haydock. In the 1460s their son Sir Piers made extensive additions to the house, including a hall with three chambers, a dining room with a kitchen, bakehouse and brewhouse, a chapel, a tower with turrets and a gatehouse. There was an older building known as the "knight's chamber" and beyond the moat lay three large barns, an oxhouse, a stable and a house for the bailiff, plus a garden and orchard. All that remains is the lowest storey of a gatehouse with a portcullis groove in the four-centred arch and tiny polygonal turrets rising from diagonal buttresses. It lies on the north side of a moated platform on which lies an 18th century house with a reset 16th century doorway.

BUCKTON RINGWORK   SD 989016

On the edge of an escarpment is an oval ringwork about 40m by 32m with a ditch around the more accessible eastern half. Gaps in the rampart face NW and SE, the latter perhaps not original. This site lies in a part of Lancashire transferred to Cheshire in 1974.

BROUGHTON TOWER

A tower at Broughton (about 5km north of Preston) here was siezed during a quarrel over its ownership in 1515. It was destroyed in 1800.

Gatehouse at Bradlegh

BURY CASTLE   SD 802108

A licence to crenellate a tower here was granted in 1465, but it was already in ruins when Leland saw it less than a century later. By that time the Stanley Earls of Derby were lords of the manor of Bury. The site lies 0.2km west of St Mary's church.

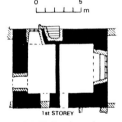

Borwick Hall: plan of tower

CLITHEROE CASTLE   SD 742416   F

The keep of Clitheroe Castle

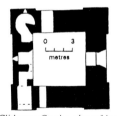

Clitheroe Castle: plan of keep

Clitheroe Castle

Clitheroe belonged to the de Lacy family and the elevated site of the castle with a rock outcrop forming a motte recalls that of their main seat at Pontefract. The keep was probably built in the 1180s by Roger de Lacy, but the castle may have existed a century earlier, there being possible references to it in documents of 1102, 1123-4 and the 1150s. Along with the other de Lacy estates Clitheroe passed on the death of Henry, Earl of Lincoln in 1311 to Thomas, Earl of Lancaster, and merged with the Crown on the accession of Henry IV in 1399. The castle was occupied in 1315 by Sir Adam Banaster in his brief rebellion against Earl Thomas. The new gateway built in 1324 was perhaps an outwork since old drawings clearly show that the now-destroyed main gatehouse at the NE corner was Norman. The deposed Henry VI was briefly kept in the castle in 1464. A new chamber was erected in 1425 and repairs were executed in 1480, but the domestic buildings were reported to be near to a state of collapse in the 1580s. The castle was occupied by Prince Rupert in 1644 but abandoned after his defeat at Marston Moor. It was ordered to be dismantled after being occupied and fortified by the Lancashire Militia when they mutined in 1649 through lack of pay. Charles II gave the site to General Monk. It was later sold to Ralph Assheton and was taken over by the Borough of Clitheroe in 1920.

The castle consists of a keep and a wedge-shaped bailey 40m wide and 90m long extending to the south. The SW corner of the bailey is an acute angle but there is no sign of a tower to strengthen it. One section of walling about 2m thick here still retains a walkway on top of it. One of the 19th century buildings in the bailey now contains a museum. Between them is the site of the chapel of St Michael, affiliated to Whalley Abbey in 1349.

The 13m high keep is 10.4m square over walls 2.6m thick. It lies within an oval court 25m across enclosed by a shell wall 2.4m thick and 2.5m high to the wall-walk, although the external height is greater. The southern part of the shell wall (which may be older than the tower keep) has been missing since at least the 16th century, and on this side the clasping pilaster buttresses on the corners of the tower have a stepped plinth dating from when it was mostly refaced in 1848. The two loops in the basement of the tower are now broken out, allowing acess. Originally the only access was by a trapdoor from above. The more thinly walled upper storey has a narrow doorway facing SW towards the shell wall-walk, but the main entrance was the doorway on the NE side, adjacent to the doorway leading to a spiral staircase ascending in the north corner. There were narrow windows facing SE and NW and a latrine chamber in the west corner. The tower then rose up another stage (with thinner walls) to protect the roof.

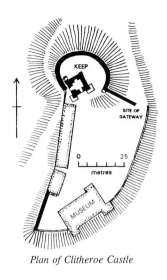

Plan of Clitheroe Castle

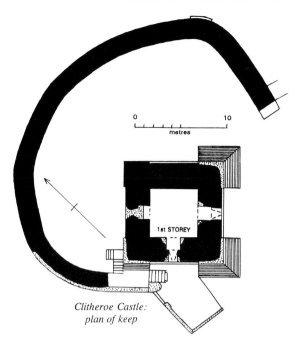

Clitheroe Castle:
plan of keep

FARLETON CASTLE

SD 578669

Excavations on a platform here revealed part of a retaining wall of cut blocks but no buildings or proper moat. This is a rather doubtful castle or manor house site.

Greenhalgh Castle

Interior of the keep at Clitheroe

Halton Castle

GREENHALGH CASTLE   SD 501451

All that remains of this castle is the lower part of a corner tower 7.4m square which seems to have been set diagonally to whatever it was attached to. It had the unusual feature of loops piercing the corners, resulting in the interior being polygonal. This weakened the structure and part, now reduced to just footings, has cracked away from the rest. The castle is said to have had a walled court and a wet moat but it is not clear whether the surviving tower formed part of that or was part of a tower house. The Stanleys were licensed by Henry VII to fortify this site in 1490. It was destroyed after capture by Parliamentary troops in 1646, following a long siege.

HALTON CASTLE   SD 500648   V

A D-shaped bailey about 40m by 30m with a ditch and rampart protects the weakest side of a motte with a summit about 9m across set on a promontory near the church.

HOGHTON TOWER   SD 622262   O

Although embattled, this late 16th century mansion with three ranges around a court and a gatehouse on the fourth side was not defensible since it has large windows near ground level, but it lies on an elevated site suitable for a fortress and the name suggests that a medieval tower either of stone or wood may have once stood here.

Castle Stede motte and bailey, Hornby

HORNBY CASTLE SD 583698 and 587685 V

The original castle here was the motte and bailey at Castle Stede beside a bridge over the River Lune. A motte with a summit about 15m across lies at the east end of a bailey platform 70m long by 60m wide with a rampart and ditch on the south side. The castle mentioned in 1205 as taken by King John from Roger de Montbegon but returned three months later was probably on this site. The later castle lies over a kilometre to the south, on a shelf above the River Wenning east of the village and parish church. Most of it is a mock Tudor fantasy created in 1849-52 by Sharpe and Paley for the financier Pudsey Dawson, but buried in the middle is a lofty early 16th century tower 11m by 9m, with a polygonal stair turret on the west side rising still higher. The irregular shape of the tower appears to be the result of later rebuilding. An old print shows the windows on the north side similar to how they are now and that the staircase was covered by a bulbous cap. Nothing then stood beyond this side of the tower. Prior to the 19th century there was a courtyard south of the tower with at least two round towers. Originally a seat of the Harringtons, the castle later passed to the Stanleys, Barons Monteagle. The daughter and heiress of the 3rd Lord Monteagle married Edmund Parker, Lord Morley, for whom James I revived the Monteagle barony. The castle was stormed by a Parliamentary force in 1644.

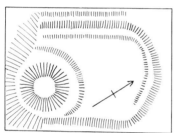

Plan of Halton Castle

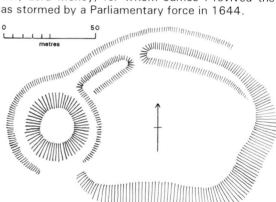

Plan of Castle Stede motte and bailey at Hornby

Greenhalgh Castle

Hornby Castle before reconstruction

Hornby Castle

Lancaster Castle, upper part of keep

*The Well Tower
(Witches Tower)
at Lancaster*

LANCASTER CASTLE   SD 473619   O

This castle was founded in 1093 by Roger de Poitou on the site of a former Roman fort. The hilltop site commanded the lowest crossing of the River Lune and also a view across Morecambe Bay to the Furness District, which along with much of modern Lancashire was given to Roger for his support of William II in a recent campaign against the Scots in which the boundary between the two countries was pushed up to Carlisle. The hilltop was big enough to not only accommodate Roger's castle but the Benedictine priory he established alongside it in 1094. Roger was forfeited by Henry I in 1102 after supporting a rebellion in favour of Robert Curthose, the eldest son of William the Conqueror, who had succeeded to the Duchy of Normandy whilst his younger brothers became in turn kings of England. Henry I eventually granted the Honour of Lancaster to his nephew Stephen of Blois. He took the throne in 1135 instead of Henry's daughter Matilda. Unable to fight both Matilda and the Scots at the same time, Stephen was obliged to let David, King of Scotland occupy Cumbria and Lancashire as far south as the Ribble. In 1154, under the terms of a treaty made the previous year, Matilda's son became King Henry II whilst Stephen's younger son William held the Honour of Lancaster until his death in 1164. Only then did the county of Lancashire come into existence. There is no record of when or by whom the keep was erected. The most likely scenarios are that it was erected by Henry I c1105-20 or by King David of Scotland in the late 1140s.

In 1189 Richard I granted the Honour of Lancaster to his younger brother John, who was forfeited for rebellion in 1194. John became king himself in 1199 and between 1209 and 1211 he spent over £630 on improving the castle. A ditch was dug around the south and west sides and work was carried out on "the King's lodgings". It is assumed that Adrian's Tower formed part of this work. John's son Henry III spent almost £200 on repairing the keep and gatehouse in 1243. The palisades mentioned at this time were probably outworks since it is likely that the main enclosure had a full set of curtain walls and towers by the end of John's reign. However, there is a record of £250 being spent on the curtain walls and gateway in 1254. The Well Tower is thought to have been rebuilt as part of repairs carried out by Edward II after a Scottish invasion of 1322. That year the Honour of Lancaster was forfeited to the Crown with the defeat and execution of the king's cousin Thomas. Edward III eventually restored the Honour to Thomas's brother Henry, whose granddaughter Blanche married the king's fourth son John of Gaunt. Edward III eventually raised all his sons to dukedoms, and in 1362 John of Gaunt thus became Duke of Lancaster, a title first granted to Blanche's father Henry in 1351.

The gatehouse of Lancaster Castle

In 1399 John of Gaunt's heir returned from exile, forced the deposition of his cousin Richard II and was crowned as Henry IV. In 1402 he began work on the present gatehouse, replacing one thought to have been damaged during a Scottish invasion in 1389. Expenditure of 200 marks a year on the castle was authorised, and by the time Henry V died in 1422 over £2500 had been spent on the building. The top storey of the keep dates mostly from this period and the other towers were remodelled. Robert Fairburn's paintings of the castle dating from 1800 clearly show the former Dungeon Tower surmounted by battlements of 15th century type. During the later medieval period the castle gradually decayed although it remained in use as a courthouse and prison for the county. Following a survey of 1578 Queen Elizabeth had the keep repaired. High up on the north side of it is a stone with the year 1585 and the initials E.R. with those of Richard Assheton, then Sheriff of Lancashire. In 1612 the great hall was the scene of the trial of the Pendle Witches, resulting in eight women and two men being hanged on Lancaster Moor. Also hanged on the moor between 1583 and 1646 were eleven Catholic priests and four other Catholic conspirators found guilty of treason at a court in the castle.

The inner face of the gatehouse at Lancaster

The castle was inadequately garrisoned by the Royalists at the start of the Civil War and consequently easily fell to a small Parliamentary force sent from Preston in February 1643. In March the Royalists stormed the earthworks newly set up at the town entrances but after besieging the castle for two days withdrew because of the threat of a relieving force from Preston. Two other unsuccessful attempts were made to retake the castle in April and June of that year. Despite orders being issued for the destruction of the curtain walls in 1645 and again in 1647 and 1649 it does not appear that they were then executed. When the Duke of Hamilton brought a Scottish army south in support of King Charles in 1648 a Parliamentary garrison was able to withstand a short siege by Royalists. The castle seems to have still been defensible when Charles II was proclaimed king at Lancaster in 1651 and the castle gates were opened and the prisoners released. However, the curtain walls had gone by 1660 when Charles II was restored. The sheriff and justices petitioned Charles II to have the buildings repaired for the holding of courts and the safe keeping of prisoners and records. A survey of December 1663 estimated that £2000 needed spending on the works. Eventually the gatehouse was repaired, along with the hall block and the southern half of the keep, which was used as the Shire Hall or civil court, debtors being kept in the room above, whilst lunatics were housed in the basement until a special asylum for them was built in 1816. The northern half of the keep seems to have been left roofless until the remodelling of the castle of the 1790s. Walls much thinner and lower than the original curtains were built to reconnect the towers to make an exercise yard. Prisoners kept at the castle during the 1660s and 70s including several Quakers, the most notable of them being their leader George Fox.

In November 1715 the Jacobite army entered Lancaster, proclaimed James III as king and set the prisoners free. Only a few weeks later four hundred Jacobites, from the army recently defeated at Preston, were incarcerated in the castle. The Lancashire Justices obtained an Act of Parliament in 1788 for the remodelling of the castle to provide more modern building both for the holding of courts and the keeping of prisoners. The first campaign of building to designs by Thomas Harrison was started immediately and completed in the early 1800s. The courts have remained in use as such ever since, although the most serious cases are now tried at Preston. The castle ceased to hold convicted criminals in 1916 and was then used for German prisoners-of-war. In the 1930s the prison was used as for training police cadets and during the war the castle was occupied by the military. In 1954 the castle again became a prison, which it remains to the present day, despite closure plans.

Lancaster Castle from the churchyard

In its present form the castle is rather larger than it was in medieval times. The Shire Hall of 1796-8 lies beyond the original hall block on the west and the prison for male felons of 1794-6 extends a further 24m out beyond the line of the vanished northern curtain wall. North and west of the gatehouse are the Gaoler's House and a prison for female felons which extend out up to 6m beyond the line of the former curtain wall. In fact the only original section of curtain wall is the western part of the south side between the site of the Dungeon Tower demolished in 1818 to make room for the new Female Penitentiary and the circular Adrian's Tower in the SW corner. Originally the south curtain continued past the four storey Dungeon Tower (which measured about 10m by 8m) for a total of about 55m from Adrian's tower before turning through a corner for a short distance to meet the gatehouse. The rest of the courtyard then formed a D-shape, extending 63m to the north from the south curtain.

Adrian's Tower has an external diameter of about 10m. It is now assumed to be early 13th century, although its name reflects an earlier belief that it was built by the Roman Emperor Hadrian. Medieval masonry survives inside it but the exterior has been refaced. In 1796 the hall block north of Adrian's Tower was demolished except for two basement rooms which were incorporated into a larger new building providing new court rooms. This is the only part open to the public. There is a round tower at the north end of this block, recalling that originally a round tower projected from the NW corner of the original hall block, which thus had an overall layout rather like that which survives in a more complete original late 13th century state at Shrewsbury.

The 12th century keep (not open to the public) measures about 22m square over walls up to 3m thick and 18m high. There are typical Norman pilaster buttresses at each corner and the middle of each side. The keep has four storeys but the topmost level seems to be 15th century work and in its original form the building may have only had two levels, with a hall and chamber with large shafted windows set above dark cellars, one of which was later used as the prison chapel. The hall lay on the south, where the entrance was, and there is a spiral stair in the SW, above which rises a turret known as John of Gaunt's Chair. The part of the prison immediately north of the keep was used for hangings which could be watched by the public from the churchyard. After public hangings were abolished in 1868 executions took place in a court east of the keep. The last execution in the castle was in 1910 but the apparatus remained until the death penalty was abolished in Britain in 1965.

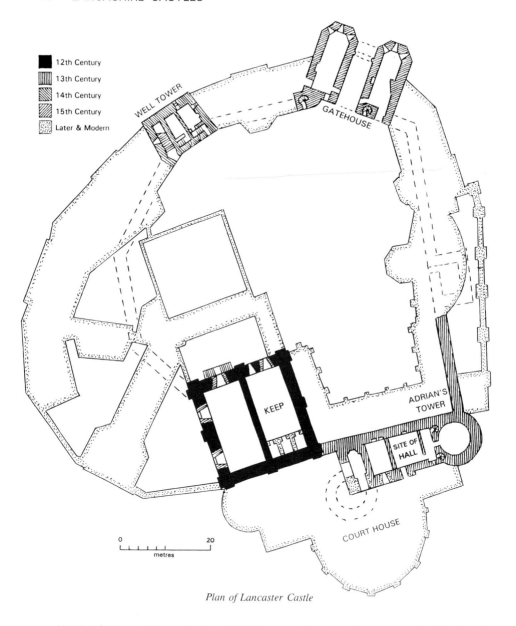

Plan of Lancaster Castle

North of the gatehouse is the Well Tower, otherwise known as the Witches' Tower, since the Pendle Witches are said to have been confined in its basement. The tower measures about 12m by 10m and has four storeys. It has an ogival-headed doorway into one of the lower rooms from the courtyard and is assumed to be a 14th century rebuilding of a structure of c1190-1216, but the battlements are of c1410. The top two storeys each retain one two-light medieval window facing the courtyard.

The gatehouse is the finest and most public remnant of the medieval castle, although its rooms are not open for inspection. It has a pair of elongated polygonal-fronted towers nearly 8m wide flanking a passageway closed by a portcullis and double doors. The gatehouse is quite forbidding externally, the three rooms on each of two upper storeys only having modest windows towards the field, whilst the guard rooms have the remains of cross-shaped arrowloops. At the summit is a machicolated parapet around the whole building except upon the NW side facing the court, where there are a few two-light upper windows. Within the parapet the other parts of the towers continue up in a square form, and attached to the inner parts of these are square turrets rising still higher. There are also square turrets over the inner corners of the building. Over the main outer archway is a niche flanked by shields. The niche contains a statue of 1822 showing John of Gaunt in armour. He was then considered the builder, although the gatehouse is now known both from records and on heraldic evidence to have been begun by his son Henry IV in 1402.

Most English county towns had defences but Lancaster is an exception. There is no certain evidence that the medieval town ever possessed either a wall or ditch.

LATHOM HOUSE   SD 459091

The Stanley family obtained this estate by marriage to the heiress of Thomas of Lathom in the late 14th century. Thomas, Lord Stanley, who held the estate from 1459 until 1504, built a huge castellated mansion with a central tower or keep, two courts, eleven other towers and a double moat. In 1485 Lord Stanley was expected to support Richard III and his change of sides at Bosworth gave a victory for the man that became Henry VII. In return he was made Earl of Derby, and he entertained Henry VII at Lathom in 1495. Held for King Charles by Lady Stanley, Countess of Derby, it withstood a siege by Parliamentary forces from Bolton and Liverpool in 1643-4 which ended when Prince Rupert advanced to Stockport. Devastated by cannon-fire, the house was finally demolished after surrendering after a second long siege. The Earl of Derby continued to resist Parliament from the Isle of Man until 1651. He was captured and executed after Charles II's defeat at Worcester. All that remains of his house is a detached chapel of the early 16th century. The only original feature is a doorway. Behind it are almhouses of about the same period. Only one service wing now remains of a later house, built in the 1720s to a designs by Giacomi Leoni in the Palladian style for the Liverpool barrister Sir Thomas Bootle.

Stanley Tower at Liverpool

Stanley Tower at Liverpool

LIVERPOOL CASTLE   SJ 343903

This castle is first mentioned in 1235 when its defences were strengthened. It stood where Derby Square now lies and was probably begun in 1232 by William de Ferrers. He inherited the borough of Liverpool, which had been founded as a port for travel to Ireland by King John, and was granted in 1229 by Henry III to Ranulph, Earl of Chester. The castle stood on a rocky knoll rising 15m above the mouth of the inlet known as the Pool which formed the harbour. It had a court about 45m square with a hall and postern on the west, a chapel on the south, a twin-towered gatehouse at the NE corner, and round towers projecting at the NW and SW corners, the latter providing private apartments. Surrounding the walls was a rock-cut ditch up to 18m wide from which a passage led out to the shore. This was an up-to-date design with similarities to King John's new castles of Limerick and Dublin in Ireland, the modest de Braose castle of Pembridge in Herefordshire, and to Earl Ranulph's new castles, especially Chartley in Staffordshire which had also recently passed to de Ferrers.

William de Ferrers' grandson Robert was forfeited by Henry III in 1266 for his support of the Earl of Leicester and Liverpool was granted to the king's younger son Edmund. In 1315, during the tenure of Edmund's son Thomas of Lancaster, the castle withstood an attack by his rebellious tenants. The castle came under Crown control after Earl Thomas was defeated and executed in 1322 by Edward II, and the king himself stayed at the castle of Liverpool in the following year. Edward III later restored the castle to Thomas's son Henry but it was again merged with the Crown on the accession of Henry's great grandson Henry IV in 1399. In later years the castle served merely as a prison and the constables often lived outside it in a nearby house. During the reign of Henry VI Sir Richard Molyneux was made Constable of the castle and Ranger of the parks of Toxteth, Croxteth and Simonswood. After these offices were made hereditary in this family a few years later the castle was strengthened by the addition of a new tower at the SE corner.

Liverpool was fortified in 1642 for King Charles by Lord Strange, who succeeded to the earldom of Derby in 1643. However the king then summoned most of Derby's troops off south and later that year Colonel Ashton was able to storm the town defences. No attempt was made the hold the castle independently. The victorious Parliamentarians then strengthened the defences, guns being mounted on the castle and a new fort with eight guns being erected at the corner of the Pool, whilst a fleet of six ships was kept in the Mersey. Prince Rupert stayed in the castle a few nights after recapturing the town in June 1644, Colonel Moore and the bulk of the garrison making a retreat after ten days fierce resistance and a heavy bombardment. However the prince was defeated at Marston Moor in July and by September Liverpool was again under siege. Desertion and mutiny amongst the mixed English and Irish Royalist garrison in late October led to the capture of the town, along with many officers and a considerable quantity of stores without bloodshed. The castle remained garrisoned during the Cromwellian Protectorate but was partly dismantled after Charles II's restoration in 1660. Lord Molyneux allowed a number of families to live in the grounds, where they were outside the jurisdiction of the townsfolk, who were annoyed by their unruly behaviour. At the revolution of 1688 Lord Molyneux, a Catholic, supported James II and filled the castle with supplies and munitions. He lost his hereditary constableship after being implicated in an attempted Jacobite rising of 1694. After Lord Derwentwater proclaimed James III at Lancaster during the 1715 Jacobite rebellion the authorities at Liverpool again refortified the town. In 1704 they had obtained from Queen Anne a lease of the castle site with permission to demolish it, but disputes with Lord Molyneux, who still had claims over the site, delayed demolition until 1725. A fishmarket and a church of St George were erected on the site. A memorial to Queen Victoria has replaced the latter.

LIVERPOOL: STANLEY TOWER   SJ 339904

Just 0.2km to the NW of the castle lay a second embattled building on the shore, Stanley Tower, for which Henry IV issued a licence to crenellate to Sir John Stanley in 1406. Sir John obtained lands here on his marriage to the heiress of Thomas of Lathom and was richly rewarded by Henry IV for his support against the rebellion of the Percies in 1403, being given, amongst other estates, the Isle of Man. Liverpool was then used as his place of embarkation when visiting Man. In 1424 the Sheriff of Lancaster only just managed to prevent a pitched battle being fought in the streets of the town between the armed bands of the deadly enemies Sir Thomas Stanley and Sir Richard Molyneux, both of whom were arrested. The townsfolk tended to support the Stanleys, since they were currently being terrorised by the Molyneux family. Old drawings show Stanley Tower as a composite structure with various wings and towers projecting from a main block with a machicolated parapet.

After the failure of the 1715 Jacobite rebellion the tower was filled with prisoners awaiting trial. Lord Derby sold the tower to William Clayton in 1737. It was then rented, and subsequently purchased, by the town corporation. Part of the building remained in use as a gaol, whilst the chapel was used as an assembly room in which dances were held. During the riot of 1775, caused when the wages of sailors on Liverpool-based ships were reduced, nine mutineers were imprisoned in Stanley Tower. An armed mob of 2,000 sailors marched to the tower, and, not being satisfied with the release of eight of the prisoners, broke into the building and released the ninth prisoner. The mob then besieged the Town Hall, bringing up cannon from their ships, and was only dispersed by bringing troops over from Manchester. In 1803 the tower contained seven cells either at street level or underground, each of which was about 2m square, contained three prisoners and was lighted and ventilated only by holes in the door. A larger room higher up contained twelve prisoners, both men and women. Debtors were lodged in a separate tower. They were provided with straw to sleep on and were allowed to hang out a bag for alms from passers by. The prisoners were exercised in a courtyard created from the former garden. A new prison in Great Howard Street was first used to contain French prisoners-of-war but after the end of the Napoleonic Wars it became a civil prison. Stanley Tower thus became redundant and tower was demolished in 1819 to permit the widening of Water Street.

Reconstruction of the appearance of Liverpool Castle

MANCHESTER CASTLE

There are mentions of a castle at Manchester in 1184-7 and 1216. The ruins noted by Leland in the 16th century were probably relics of the Roman fort.

MELLING MOTTE   SD 599712   V

A motte with a summit about 12m across lies on a knoll east of the church.

MOURHOLME CASTLE   SD 516724

Here probably stood the castle of Morhull or Mirhull which was surrendered to King John in 1216.

NEWTON-LE-WILLOWS: CASTLE HILL   SJ 596962

Excavations found evidence that this mound on a promontory above a river and lake may have been a barrow originally, later adapted as a motte.

PENWORTHAM CASTLE   SD 524291   F

NE of the church is a motte backed against an east facing slope. There was a tiny bailey on the north and another on the west. The castle is mentioned in Domesday Book as a recent construction. Excavation in 1856 showed that the mound had a central wooden structure around a central post and a cobbled floor prior to being heightened on two separate occasions.

The motte at Penwortham

Radcliffe Tower

PRESTON CASTLE   SD 512032

The last remains of a motte and bailey in the grounds of Tulketh Hall were destroyed in 1855. The site must have been abandoned by 1123, when the vill was given to the Cistercians to establish a monastery which later moved to Furness.

RADCLIFFE TOWER   SD 798075   F

This ruin lying on open land west of the church measures 15m by 8.5m over walls 1.5m thick above a plinth. The lowest level had a vault which collapsed in the mid 19th century, and is assumed to have been a kitchen since it has three fireplaces, one of which is now blocked up. There are two loops facing east and one towards the west. The doorway (with a draw-bar slot) in the middle of the west side faced a timber-framed hall which was demolished c1840, having become too delapidated even to keep cows in. From this hall opened the stair in the southern part of the west wall of the tower which gave access to a private living room. This room is now very ruinous but has traces of a south loop and a west fireplace. The Radcliffe family, the chief of which was always styled "of Radcliffe Tower", obtained from Henry IV a licence to crenellate a tower here in 1403. The licence mentions a second tower, probably another embattled stone cross-wing at the west end of the hall. In 1592 the Earl of Derby sent a group of recusant widows to be imprisoned at Radcliffe Tower.

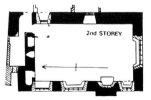

Plans of Turton Tower   *Plan of Radcliffe Tower*

Turton Tower, Lancashire

ROCHDALE CASTLE   SD 892128

The motte of this strongly sited motte and bailey castle has now gone. The only reference to the castle is in 1322, in a context which indicates the site had been abandoned long ago.

THURLAND CASTLE   SD 611731

Of the castle which Henry IV licensed Sir Thomas Tunstall to crenellate in 1402 there remain the moat facing the approach and parts of the masonry of the north range and the SE range, from which projects a tower about 6m square. The two ranges meet at an acute angle capped by a rectangular tower 12m by 8.5m with a staircase turret on the outer angle. Facing the court is an ogival-headed doorway, a feature suggesting that the castle existed at least a generation or two before the licence to crenellate. The castle was captured by Parliamentary troops in 1643. The North family made modifications and additions in 1810 and 1826-9, but the castle was gutted by a fire in 1876 and much of what now stands is the work of Paley and Austin from 1879 to 1885. The result is partly Elizabethan and partly Gothic.

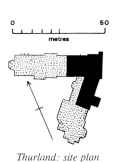

Thurland: site plan

The east side of Thurland Castle

TURTON TOWER SD 731152 O

This building consists of a tower house 13m long by 8.5m wide over walls up to 1.4m thick, a 16th century range at right angles to it containing a kitchen, and other rooms in the re-entrant angle between them, where there is an entrance hall with a chapel above and a scale-and-platt staircase. The top storey of the old tower appears to be a late 16th century addition, with the mullioned windows one might expect of that period. The two lower storeys, now the dining room and drawing room, also have inserted mullioned windows, there being a tier of five-light examples in the south end wall. What is now the upper part of the drawing room formed the medieval top storey. The northern corners have projecting turrets which contained latrines and a former spiral staircase. The tower may be of 14th century origin although it is more likely it was built by William Orrel c1430 after his marriage to the heiress Elizabeth de Torboc. The cost of the Elizabethan remodelling got the Orrels into debt and in 1628 William Orrel sold Turton to Humphrey Chetham, although he remained in residence as a tenant until 1648. In the 18th century Turton passed to Edward Chetham of Nuthurst who leased the tower to tenant farmers. It then passed to the Greene family, who in 1835 sold the tower to James Kay, a local mill owner. He carried out considerable alterations and repairs. In 1890 the tower was sold to Elizabeth and Anne Appleton, who leased it to William Rigg. In 1903 the tower was sold yet again to Sir Lees Knowles. His widow presented the tower to the local District Council in 1930. It is now administered by the Borough of Blackburn.

WARRINGTON CASTLE SJ 616885

A castle here is mentioned in 1228. By 1908 the motte and bailey site had been very damaged by building on the site and nothing now remains visible. Excavations in 1832 revealed a well lined with horizontal staves set against four corner posts and a coin of Henry III was found at a higher level.

WEST DERBY SJ 397935

At the west end of Croxteth Park, NW of West Derby church, are the last traces of a motte and bailey castle, all that survived destruction in 1817. The motte had a double ditch. Work on the castle is mentioned in 1197 and 1218-25, but by 1297 it was regarded as no more than the site of a castle and capital messuage. Excavations in 1927 and 1956 revealed parts of a timber bridge and mid 13th century pottery.

WHITTINGTON   SD 600763

The churchyard occupies the site of a motte and bailey castle of which little remains.

GLOSSARY OF TERMS

ASHLAR - Masonry of blocks with even faces and square edges.   BAILEY - Defensible court enclosed by a stone wall or a palisade and ditch. BASTION - A projection rising no higher than the curtain wall. CRENEL - A cut-way part of a parapet. Corbel - A projecting bracket to support other stonework or a timber beam. CURTAIN WALL - A high enclosing wall around a bailey. GOTHICK - An imitation late medieval style of c1740-1830. HOARDING - Wooden gallery at a wall top providing machicolations. KEEP - A citadel or ultimate strongpoint. The term is not medieval and such towers were then called donjons, from which is derived the word dungeon, meaning a prison. LIGHT - A compartment of a window. LOOP - A small opening to admit light or for the discharge of missiles. MACHICOLATION - A slot for dropping or firing missiles at assailants. MERLONS - The upstanding portions of a parapet. MOAT - A defensive ditch, either water filled or dry. MOTTE - A steep sided flat-topped mound, partly or wholly man made. MULLION - A vertical member dividing the lights of a window. PARAPET - A wall for protection at any sudden drop. PLINTH - The projecting base of a wall. It may be battered (sloped) or steeped. PORTCULLIS - A wooden gate made to rise and fall in vertical grooves, being hoisted by a windlass above. POSTERN - A back entrance or lesser gateway. RINGWORK - An embanked enclosure of more modest size than a bailey, generally of great width but less elevated than a motte summit. SCALE-AND-PLATT STAIRCASE - Staircase with short straight flights and turns at landings. SOLAR - A private living room for the lord of a castle and his family. STRONGHOUSE - A mansion difficult to break into or burn down because of its solid walls with grilles or bars on vulnerable windows, and perhaps also the presence of a moat. WALL-WALK - A walkway on top of a wall, protected by a parapet. WARD - A stone walled defensive enclosure.

PUBLIC ACCESS TO THE SITES

E Buildings in the care of English Heritage. Fee payable at some sites.
F Sites to which there is access at any reasonable time.
O Buildings opened to the public by private owners, local councils, National Trust
V Buildings closely visible from public roads, paths, churchyards and open spaces.

FURTHER READING

Castellarium Anglicanum, D.Cathcart-King 1983
Norman Castles in Britain, Derek Renn, 1968
The Walls of Chester, F.Simpson. 1910
Castles of Cheshire, P.W.Cullen & R.Hordern, 1986
Victoria County History of Cheshire (several volumes) various dates
Victoria County History of Lancashire (several volumes) various dates
A History of the County Palatine and City of Chester, G.Ormerod, 1882
Journal of the Chester Archaeological Society.
Journal of the Lancashire & Cheshire Antiquarian Society.
History of the King's Works, H.M.Colvin, 1963
Guide books are available for Beeston, Halton, Lancaster and Turton.
Transactions of The Historical Society of Lancashire and Cheshire.
See also Country Life and various Cheshire Community Council publications.